My Year with Harry Potter

My Year with Harry Potter

How I Discovered
My Own Magical World

Ben Buchanan

LANTERN BOOKS
NEW YORK

2001
Lantern Books
One Union Square West, Suite 201
New York, NY 10003

Printed in the United States of America

Library of Congress Cataloguing-in-Publication Data

Buchanan, Ben.
My year with Harry Potter : how I discovered my own magical world /
Ben Buchanan
p. cm.
ISBN 1-930051-50-6 (alk. paper)
1. Board games—Design and construction—Juvenile literature.
2. Potter, Harry (Fictitious character) —Miscellanea—Juvenile
literature. [1. Buchanan, Ben. 2. Inventors. 3. Board games—Design and
construction. 4. Rowling, J.K.—Characters—Miscellanea.
5. Children's writing. 6. Children's art] I. Title.

GV1312 .B84 2001
794'.092—dc21
[B]
2001029463

for J. K. Rowling,
she has made my imagination expand
three times its size!

Contents

Illustrations

1.
Harry Flies into My Life

Ben Buchanan of 814 Grinnell Drive was proud to say that he had a mystical life, thank you very much. "I'm normal," Ben says, "but I'm not normal." Well, let's let him tell the story:

I'm normal because I am a normal kid—going to school, being happy, getting homework, having a family.

I'm not normal because I'm dyslexic. I have a scar on my head. I'm not normal because mystical things happen to me.

Take the day I received my first Harry Potter book. It was Christmas of my fourth grade year. The books weren't really famous then, and I didn't know anything about Harry Potter. But there was a present on the couch next to my Christmas stocking. I picked up the book and I thought: "This looks good. I want to read it!"

Later that day, my mother started reading it to me. Hearing the first chapter, I could tell that it sounded like my type of book—a fantasy or science fiction book. It looked like an exciting book and it got more exciting as it went along. Pretty soon, I didn't want my mom to read it to me because I wanted to read it myself.

My life started to change at Christmas. My life changed because when Harry Potter flew into it, I met him and I wanted to learn about him and I wanted to bring him to life. I wanted more.

The life that Harry flew into was a life full of rabbits and dragons and happiness and magic.

My family takes care of lost or mistreated bunnies. The first rabbit was for my brother because he read *Watership Down* five times and then every book in the library about rabbits. We named her Holly after a character in *Watership Down*. The next rabbit was for me, and I named her Silver. I named her Silver because she was gray, but my brother Doug said it was after *Watership Down*, too. Two more rabbits joined us, one for my mom, who was named Leia (after *Star Wars*) and one for my dad. He named the rabbit Domino for two reasons. One, because he was black and white and the other for the domino effect—since one person had called another person who had called my mom to find out if we could take another homeless bunny. This one had been hopping around some busy streets in Dallas.

About my scar. I got my scar when I was about the age that Harry got his. And like Harry, it involved being given into the care of strangers. But in my case it was for surgery. A bump on my forehead right near where Harry's scar is had been discovered. (It was a "dermoid cyst.") The doctors were concerned it might grow into my brain and so surgery was necessary. But in order that I not have a scar on my forehead, like Harry does, they made a big headband cut. So I have a scar from one ear to the other. Mostly my hair covers it. But when I go swimming it is pretty obvious. The scar means I can't get certain haircuts…or at least I'm not ready to do that yet. One of my friend's mothers suggested that I could use a magic marker and color the scar whatever color I wanted. Maybe I will someday!

For many years I didn't really understand why I had that scar. I guess my parents had told me but I hadn't understood. So I often told kids I had been in a car accident. That's how so many terrible things happen and that's what I thought I had been told. So I guess like Harry I didn't at first understand why I had a scar.

My brother, Doug, likes to draw a lot, like me. He likes to draw dragons. He draws dragons everywhere—on his homework, on scraps of paper, and in sketchbooks. His math teacher in ninth grade always knew which was his homework, even if he forgot to put his name on the sheet of paper. There were dragons everywhere. This made me interested in fantasy. I could understand why Hagrid would want to have a dragon.

My life is wonderful. It's not mythical because nothing with real dragons and real unicorns happens to me. But it's mystical because my life is a mystery and strange things happen in it. Magical things happen. My year with Harry Potter was a magical year. Let me tell you about it.

2.
Reading Harry Potter

I am dyslexic. Dyslexia means having difficulty reading. For me dyslexia has meant that from the middle of second grade until the end of third grade, I was pulled out of my regular class to go to a special tutor who taught me how to read. Because of dyslexia, I had to learn things most kids take for granted.

I remember that I didn't think I was going to the tutor because of my dyslexia; I thought I was going there to learn cursive. I didn't like leaving class because I enjoyed reading. I just wasn't good at it.

Sometimes I forget that I ever had trouble reading at all. But the feelings I had when I couldn't read were, well, upsetting and weird. They were weird because I wasn't used to not being able to do something I wanted to do. And yet with reading, I wanted to read, but I couldn't. I remember in first grade I couldn't even read a word like "cookies." I remember I couldn't pronounce it. When I pronounced it wrong, my teacher corrected me and I thought, "how come the other kids don't have problems like this?" I knew the word cookie and I used the word cookie (and I ate cookies!). But looking at the letters that spelled cookie, I could not tell what the word was.

I remember that for summer vacation after first grade, if we read for twenty hours and kept a chart, we would have a pizza party when school started. I really liked pizza but it was hard for me to read, and I was worried whether I would be able to read twenty hours. Now, twenty hours would be easy, especially when I'm reading J. K. Rowling, Philip Pullman, or Lewis Carroll.

In second grade, I knew I wasn't good at reading because I was in the lowest reading group. The teacher would say "go into your reading group" and, though she never said it was the lowest, I could tell because of the size of the books that different groups were reading. In the lowest reading group we were reading *Frog and Toad*. In the medium group they were reading *I Was a First Grade Werewolf*. The highest reading group was reading *George's Marvelous Medicine*.

There were only three people in my reading group. My friends wanted to be in the easy reading group because they thought their books were too hard. I wanted to be in the harder reading group because I didn't like being in my group. I wanted to be reading other books.

One of my predictions for the New Year when I was in second grade was "I'll start third grade and not be held back by my reading. I'll get better at my reading." In the middle of second grade, I must have been really concerned about this, because my other predictions were not quite so serious—they were about going to more garage sales with my father.

My father and I have a Saturday ritual of going to garage sales on those Saturdays when he isn't working. We start off in our neighborhood and go to others. One time when we were looking for garage sales, we were looking for one that was on Grove Street. I thought you spelled Grove "G-r-o-v." But we were on a street that said G-r-o-v-e and I thought we were on a street called "Grover." My dad hadn't noticed that we were on Grove. I said, "Well, we are on Grover. How far away is Grove from Grover?" I guess that is an example of my dyslexia.

But, although I'm dyslexic, I love words! In third grade at the end of the school year, we had to do a report on an "ology"—like Egyptology or vulcanology or zoology. I really liked myths, so I wanted to do mythology. But my teacher said that I already knew a lot about myths, so she encouraged me to do something else. I decided to do a report on etymology, which means the study of the history of words. J. K. Rowling seems interested in words, too. I love to read the words she has made up: Quidditch, Azkaban, Diagon, Quaffle.

By the time I got to fourth grade, two things had happened. The first thing was that I had learned how to read through the special tutoring. And I'd done it just in time! Because the second thing that happened was that *Harry Potter and the Sorcerer's Stone* was published. When I got Harry Potter for Christmas, all the other kids thought it was just another one of those books I read because I had brought big books to school before.

But this Harry Potter book wasn't just another book. It was *the* best book that I had read. I wanted everyone else to have a chance to read it, so I spent my March allowance and bought a copy for my teacher to read to the class.

By that summer, another Harry Potter book was out. I bought this one in Santa Fe when we were on vacation. I finished it in three days because it was so suspenseful. But I still thought the first book was better. The third book in the Harry Potter series was lent to me by my school librarian at the end of summer vacation. It wasn't out in the United States yet, but she had a British copy. I took real good care of it because it wasn't my copy. I thought *this* was the best book I had ever read.

As I was reading it, I told my mother, "I can tell two things about J. K. Rowling: She is a Christian and she isn't a vegetarian." I knew this because there wasn't much vegetarian food at Hogwarts, unlike some vegetarian places in fantasy books, like Tom Bombadil's house in J. R. R. Tolkien's *Lord of the Rings* and Medwyn's Hidden Valley in Lloyd Alexander's *The Book of Three*. I knew J. K. Rowling was Christian because Kwanzaa and Hanukah and Ramadan weren't celebrated at Hogwarts.

When the American copy of the third book came out, I read it and reread it and reread it again.

Reading Harry Potter was easy. Getting up to the point of being able to read it was not. If I hadn't known how to read, Harry Potter might have flown right past my life.

3.

The Game Begins

At my school there is a yearly competition called the "Invention Convention." When I was in third grade I entered a *two-th* brush. It was a toothbrush that had a toothbrush attached to it, so that it would brush both sides of your teeth at once. I got third place in the Invention Convention. In fourth grade, I entered a dice roller. When you pushed a button, it would roll the dice that it contained so you could make sure there wasn't any cheating in the dice rolling of your friends. I got second place in the Invention Convention.

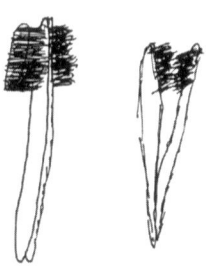

On New Year's Day, 1999, just seven days after I had received my first Harry Potter book, I made these predictions:

- "I will try to turn 10." (That was a joke...)
- "Try to convince Zein and Keaton that paper is not two-dimensional."
- "I predict that I'm going to win first place in the Invention Convention."

My friends Zein and Keaton thought that paper was two-dimensional because when you turned it sideways, you couldn't see it. But I thought it was three-dimensional because when you piled it up it had depth. If paper was two-dimensional then a book would be almost invisible when on its side, and yet books weren't. But at first Zein and Keaton weren't convinced by my logic. We argued during school about this. I wanted my brother, Doug, to come to school and explain to them that paper was three-dimensional because they wouldn't listen to me. Finally, around spring, I convinced them, and my prediction came true.

But my other prediction—winning the Invention Convention—wouldn't be as easy to achieve. Every year, my close friend Zein has beaten me. In third grade, he won second, when I won third. In fourth grade, he won first, when I won second. I decided at New Year's that this year would be the year I would win. When I made that prediction on New Year's, I didn't know then that I would be creating a Harry Potter game, but I knew I wanted to win first place.

Zein always has inventions that have to do with storage. In second grade, he invented a clipboard that attached erasers, pencils, pens, markers, rulers, scissors (everything that you needed) to the clipboard and it was called "the Magic Clipboard." He won second place. In third grade, he did the "kid safe key chain." In fourth grade, he made a "baby seat safety protection"—an invention for the seat belt of babies in car seats so they couldn't get out.

In planning for the next Invention Convention, I thought about what I would enter. I had lots of ideas. During the summer, my favorite idea was "the flying shoe." This was a shoe that would have a really strong north magnet on it facing downward and the sidewalk would have a really strong north magnet on it facing upward. The two magnets would repel each other and you would be able to walk on the air. The problem with this idea was there wasn't a magnet that had a really strong one side (north) and a really weak other side (south). I needed magnets this way so that the magnets would repel and you wouldn't hit your head on the sidewalk from the force of the pull of the magnet. So I began to think of other ideas.

By this time, school had begun. I was reading the third Harry Potter book, while my teacher was reading the first Harry Potter to the class. This was interesting because some kids were meeting Harry Potter for the first time, while a few of us had already read it. I enjoyed hearing the story again, because it is filled with such imagination.

Before the Invention Convention, we have something called "Crazy Hat Day." Each of us in my class helped to make a hat for the superintendent of the Richardson

Independent School District. I also made a "thinking" hat that was silver and had a picture of a light bulb on it. You know how, in cartoons and comics when someone gets an idea, a light bulb appears above their head? Well, my dad had gotten a thing at a garage sale that when you pushed the button, an arm would rise up and a light bulb at the end lit up and went "ding!" I fastened that to my hat.

When it's Crazy Hat Day, you know that the Invention Convention is only a month away. So that's when most kids start to work on their inventions. My teacher was reading the first Harry Potter book, my mother was reading the second Harry Potter book to me, and I had just finished the third. I also was listening to the first book on tape. Harry Potter filled my life.

Meanwhile, I was experiencing some frustration in my life. This frustration had to do with my other love: Monopoly™. I really liked to play Monopoly™. But my friends did not like to play it. And my family was pretty tired of playing it. Sometimes I would play it with my mother as she cooked dinner, but I didn't like that because she kept on cooking rather than playing.

So there it was: the Invention Convention was looming. Harry Potter was all around my thoughts, and I couldn't get anyone to play my favorite game. What was I going to do?

I'd like to say an owl arrived suggesting I make a Harry Potter Board Game. But that is not what happened. Nor did Hagrid show up with a letter from Professor Dumbledore. But something just as magical happened one day and I don't know how and I don't know when, but suddenly I just knew what I could do. A light bulb went off in my head!

I realized I could make a Harry Potter Monopoly™

game! I picked the name of my game by thinking about what you could call the money—since you would be trying to get money—but not call it "money." I thought of treasure! Why not treasure? I would call it "Harry Potter and the Search for the Lost Treasure"!

But then something even more exciting happened: As I thought about the endless possibilities for it, the game took on a life of its own and became its very own game. The treasure I was really talking about turned out to be something other than money. It was within me.

In creating the game, my life came together. It was as though Harry Potter used his "Repairo" Spell. I'm not saying my life was broken, but I am saying that my life got better. All the things I loved to do—like go to garage sales and work with my hands—became part of the game. The world that I lived in and the world that I imagined started to become one.

4.
Planning

Where to begin? One of the requirements of the Invention Convention is to keep an Inventor's Journal, in which you would keep notes about the progress of your invention. You needed to record what went through your head when you were planning the invention.

Every day at school before we switched class, I would sketch in my journal and write in it. I was planning what the board would look like. I also wrote down my thoughts, what I did every day on the invention, my progress toward completing the invention, what I would have on the spaces, and what type of characters and what kind of challenges there would be.

First, I thought of places from the Harry Potter books that would become spaces. I decided on spaces like:

- *Gringotts*
- *Hagrid's Shack*
- *Flourish and Blotts.*

Since Flourish and Blotts was a bookstore, I added that you could buy your own Harry Potter book for five Galleons. The Harry Potter book would give you the opportunity to use it to help you with trivia questions I included with my game.

As I got involved in thinking about places in Harry Potter that could be spaces on my board, I was able to make them more complicated by adding commands or directions. For instance, there was a space that said:

- *You mess up going to Diagon Alley with Floo powder. Go to the Dursleys*
  Or
- *Visit Hagrid's shack in the Forbidden Forest*

I wanted a lot of the exciting interactions that were in the books to be in the game, too. So I made *them* into spaces:

- *There is a Dementor behind you. Go ahead 7 spaces*
- *You ate too many chocolate frogs. Go back 5 spaces*
- *Quidditch practice takes up too much time. Go back 5 spaces.*
- *Go to Azkaban*
- *Norbert comes to visit you. Lose one turn.*

Then I found myself imagining things that *could* happen, but had never happened in the books. These, too, I made into squares. For instance,

- *The Time-Turner takes you to visit Hagrid in Azkaban. Go to Azkaban.*

That never happened in any of the books for several reasons: Harry never went to Azkaban; the only place the Time-Turner took people in the books was back in time; and the only person who had the Time-Turner was Hermione and she never went to Azkaban either!

As I imagined a board, I also created spaces that involved money, so that people would gain or lose money as they went around the board. For instance,

- *Lose 2 Galleons*
- *Find 20 Sickles*
- *Find 2 Galleons*
- *Lose 7 Sickles*
- *Find 9 Sickles*

I wrote in my inventor's logbook whenever I had an idea. Sometimes it was at school, because I had time to work on it. But sometimes it was in the car when I was riding somewhere. I also talked about my ideas with my family.

By the time I was ready to start making the board, I had a lot done. In fact, I had decided to have not one board, nor even two boards, but three (!) boards. At this point, I was ready for the first task.

5.
The First Task
(Creating the First Board)

The First Task was not to get the Golden Egg, but was to create the first board—the Hogwarts' Board. I knew immediately what I would use: I would take a game board from a different game that I had gotten at a garage sale and spray paint it. I spray painted this board scarlet red. I picked red because it is the color of Gryffindor. While it was drying I thought about what I could put on the spaces and how I could decorate it.

I went to my closet. There I grabbed a bag full of things to decorate a dollhouse that I had gotten at a garage sale. In this bag was wallpaper, colored aluminum foil, and small shingles for roofing the dollhouse. I considered the possibilities, and I thought I could cut out the shiny aluminum foil—red, gold, blue, and silver—in the shapes of gems to decorate the board, since my game was called Harry Potter and the Search for the Lost Treasure.

I drew the shapes of the gems using a compass. I made different sizes of gems and different shapes. By pressing hard enough with the compass, I cut the shapes of the gems out.

Now my board was dry. I glued the shapes onto the middle of the board. Then I started painting the squares onto the board around the edges. I used paint that I had gotten from a paint by numbers kit that Christmas.

At the church that my dad works at there was a board game called Mystery Mansion that had trap doors, treasure chests, and was a game like Clue. When I was going through it one day, I realized I could use these for my Harry Potter game. The board game was missing pieces from it and it was going to be thrown away because it couldn't be played. So I asked my dad if I could have some things from it and he said yes.

I glued the five trap doors on five spaces and gave them each a number. I glued the three stairs on three spaces, and opposite them I put the remaining three stairs so that if you landed on one you would go straight across to the other side. The treasure chests were always next to the stairs. I decided that the way they would work in my game was that if you landed on the staircase place then you would move directly across from the space you were on to the other space. If you landed on the trap door space you would roll the six-sided dice and the number you got would send you to the trap door with that number. Since there were only five trap doors, if you got a six you would reroll the dice. So, for instance, if you rolled a five then you would go to trap door number five.

The treasure chests had either a spider in them or a picture of money. I decided the spider would be Aragog, from Harry Potter Book Two. If you landed on a treasure chest and you decided to open it and Aragog was in it, then you would lose one Galleon. However, if you landed on the treasure chest and you opened it and there was treasure in it, you would gain one Galleon.

But here I encountered my first problem. My handwriting was too messy and too big to fit into the little spaces that were on my board for each square. Nor would my pen write on the paint. It didn't even smear. It simply would not write on the bright shiny red paint I had so carefully painted on the board.

I had thought about what the squares would say so carefully and now I couldn't get the commands onto the board! So my mom and I had the idea that we could type the commands onto labels and then put the labels onto the squares. This worked great! Each label fit into the square and was legible. My game was saved from my own handwriting! After about a week's work, my first task was accomplished. And I didn't even have to beat a dragon from Hungary!

6.
The Second Task (The Second Board)

Azkaban weighs heavily on the rocks that support it on its island. Azkaban weighed heavily on me, as well. What a dreary, stony, evil, unhappy, Dementory, isolated, terrifying, sickly place! Yet I wanted to create it and have it in my game. Dreariness is part of life. It's part of my life, part of my mom's life, my brother's life, and my father's life. For instance, some of our rabbits have gotten murdered by other creatures. When my rabbits died, I felt sad and upset. I felt what it must feel like to be at Azkaban—desolated. So Azkaban was like a magnet to me—it attracted me and it repelled me.

I knew I was going to do an Azkaban board because I wanted my game to be like Monopoly™ and Azkaban is a jail. I didn't make it a space on my Hogwarts board. Instead, I wanted it to be a board that would be three-dimensional, like the other boards I was making.

So I started to work. First I cut a piece of cardboard that was about ten inches wide by six inches long. I started to spray paint it blue since Azkaban is an island. But then the blue spray paint ran out. So I decided to spray paint it silver instead. I gathered about five big rocks from my back yard and I glued them with hot glue onto the board. I had dried lichen I had bought from a hobby store and glued some onto the rocks. Next, I got cardboard pieces that looked like a ruined castle from a game (Warhammer™) that my brother and I used to play. I glued these pieces onto the rocks and I arranged them to look like a fortress.

The only bad thing about the Azkaban board is that it is too heavy. Sometimes, when I move the board, the rocks tumble off. At first I just let them fall off, but later I started bringing tape in the box that held the game so I could fix it.

I put a space on the Hogwarts board that said, "As you pass, go to Azkaban." You had to stay in Azkaban until you paid two Sickles. Then you would get to go to the third board, the Forbidden Forest. I know my Azkaban is different than in the Harry Potter books. But when you think about why someone goes to Azkaban in the Harry Potter books those reasons don't always make sense (like Hagrid being sent to Azkaban). I made my Azkaban different because I couldn't think of a way that you could suffer a sentence of being sent to Azkaban such as I found in the Harry Potter books. So I made Azkaban less frightening, time-consuming, dangerous, and threatening. Instead, I made it something that each player would go to and then escape from. I made Azkaban the way I wanted to and it makes the game more challenging.

7.
The Third Task
(The Third Board)

The Forbidden Forest is an enchanted, dangerous place. Magical things happen there. I decided to create the Forbidden Forest because of the kind of magic there. In the Forbidden Forest, magic was not simply evil, like Azkaban, nor odd, like Hogwarts. This magic was dangerous but fascinating. It drew you in, like a path in the woods. There was a lot of mystery in the forest. It had unexpected turns everywhere. If someone entered there, that person would not know what would happen.

To capture this feeling of mystery I decided my Forbidden Forest board would feature quiz cards. A winding, magical path would lead to Hagrid's shack and there would be mystical waterfalls that held money-giving quiz cards behind their watery curtain.

First, I took an old board from a Duck Tale's board game and spray painted it green. Next, I painted the squares that would be on it with the same paint I used for the squares on the Hogwarts Board. The squares made a path of magic through the forest. Then, I labeled a space "Hagrid's Shack." I used the same lichen I'd used before, and plastic trees. I had made the trees earlier, about two years ago, for a different project. But now these trees seemed perfect for the Forbidden Forest. I glued the lichen and the trees to the board, and also glued some lichen to the trees. I glued them in such a way that the board could still be partially folded.

Because I like answering questions, I created quiz cards. I constructed and painted a three-dimensional waterfall. I used cardboard, glue, and many shades of blue paint. I made it so that it could hold the quiz cards. The quiz cards would actually go behind the waterfall. And the answers would sit on top of it.

The path through the Forbidden Forest splits into two directions. One direction is longer but has better squares on it than the shorter one. The long way provides the opportunity to find money. But both paths lead to the same place, which is the middle of the board where you are supposed to draw a quiz card. You draw the quiz card and someone asks you the question. If you get it correct you get the money. Then you go back to Start on the Hogwarts Board. If you get it wrong, you don't get any money. Instead, you have to pay five Sickles to each of the other players. Then you go back to Start on the Hogwarts board. It's kind of like life: You win some, you lose some, but you are always trying again. And the place you are going to start from is at the beginning.

8.
Exams

Each year at Hogwarts, Harry has to take end-of-year exams. I thought the players should have to take exams, too. The quiz cards were their exams.

It was fun to think of the questions. I thought of some of the easiest things that I knew about the books and some of the hardest things. Like how many Sickles in a Galleon, and how many Knuts are in five Galleons. I would look back at the books to get some ideas and to make sure the answers were correct. I decided that getting right the challenging questions would give you more money than the easier ones. For each question I put how many Galleons you would get. I printed them out from the computer on labels. Then I pasted them onto three-by-five index cards.

For the answers, I either already knew them or I looked back at the book. I printed the answers out and put them on a different colored index card. Each question and each answer was numbered so that the question that was on the number one card would have its answer on the number one answer card.

Although I did not divide the questions by which book

they appear in, if I were doing this again I would probably color code the questions to the books. For instance, Book One would be pink, and Book Four would be green. That way, if I were playing with someone who hadn't read all the books, we would only play with the color quiz card that she or he has read. I decided not to use trick questions or unanswerable questions, like "What does Madame Pomfrey teach?", "What house was Hagrid in?", or "How did Hagrid's dad die?"

These are the quiz card questions I came up with. Of course, you could make up a lot more.

1. *Name all of the Weasleys' sons in the order in which they were born.*
2. *How many Knuts are in five Galleons?*
3. *Can Neville Longbottom bounce?*
4. *Why is Dudley's first television broken?*
5. *What flavor Bertie Bott's Every Flavor bean did Dumbledore get at the end of Book One?*
6. *What is Bill's job?*
7. *How many Knuts are in one Sickle?*
8. *What vault is the Sorcerer's Stone in?*
9. *What platform do you go to to get on the Hogwarts Express?*
10. *What do kids at Hogwarts think the job "defense against the dark arts" is?*
11. *Who are Harry's parents?*
12. *Who is Voldermort?*
13. *What is the Weasleys' house called?*
14. *What potion lets you change into another person?*
15. *What position does Alicia Spinnet play?*
16. *What type of broom did Malfoy get for his team?*

17. *Who is Marcus Flint?*
18. *What was the Malfoy's old house elf named?*
19. *What is Dumbledore's first name?*
20. *Where is Honeydukes?*
21. *Who is Scabbers?*
22. *What is a Pocket Sneakoscope?*
23. *What is the Marauder's Map?*
24. *Who is Harry's godfather?*
25. *What is Buckbeak?*
26. *Who are James Potter's three best friends?*
27. *What do you have to do to open the "Monster Book of Monsters"?*
28. *Who is Harry's overall favorite teacher?*

Too bad all the tests that we have to take don't have questions like this!

9.
Wizards and Witches

I wanted my playing pieces to be three-dimensional. The obvious thing to do was to use characters from the Harry Potter books as the playing pieces. Harry, Ron, Hermione, and Malfoy would be the tokens. In order for them to be three-dimensional, I decided to use clay. My brother was really, really good at making creatures with Sculpey Clay, so I decided to give it a try.

First I made Harry. Using colored clay, I made brown balls that I shaped into ovals for shoes. I made blue pants, a red shirt, hands, and a head. I gave him black hair, blue eyes, a nose, a mouth, and a scar. Making the first figure took the longest because I didn't know in advance how I was going to make them. It was a matter of experimenting with the clay.

Then I made Ron—tall and lanky as J. K. Rowling describes him. I shaped the clay the same way except that Ron had brown shoes, dark blue pants, a dark blue shirt, red hair, and blue eyes. I made Hermione next. She had brown shoes, a red skirt, a green shirt. I put a red bow in Hermione's hair.

I made a green base upon which the characters stand. They are each approximately two inches tall though Ron is the tallest and Hermione is the shortest.

Finally, I made Malfoy. I wanted an evil person in the game. I chose Malfoy for a couple of reasons: I didn't know how to make Voldermort and I wanted all the characters to be kids. As I made Malfoy, I thought about how different the Harry Potter books would be if he wasn't in them. Book Two would never have happened. As I worked with the clay, I gave Malfoy an unhappy look on his face. I think Malfoy is evil enough that he deserves to be unhappy. So that's why I gave him an unhappy expression.

I think another reason I included Malfoy is because there have been Malfoys in my life—not just annoying kids, but sometimes mean, hurtful, painful, threatening, and dangerous kids.

Some kids have made fun of me because I'm a vegetarian. The worst time was in first grade. I didn't know what to do. There have been bullies in my life, too. One took my desserts. He would ask if he could have my dessert and I gave it to him every time he asked because he was a bully. I didn't know what else to do. He was a Malfoy at that time, because if I told on him he would say that I gave them to him. I felt trapped.

I've dreamt about Malfoy, too. I had a nightmare that Malfoy was trying to get me, and when I woke up it seemed so real that I got a rubber band, put it on my fingers, pulled it back, and had it ready to release. I heard footsteps coming and I thought it was Malfoy. I said, "I'm warning you, I'm armed." Then I came back to reality. My mom was standing there. She had come to check on me.

For all these reasons, I included Malfoy. Making Malfoy

didn't change my feelings about bullies. But if I wanted to, I could drop the Malfoy character and break it. I don't want to hurt my game, so I haven't; but a part of me thinks I should because it might make me feel better against bullies.

10.
Gringotts

When I made my game, I knew that I was going to have to make money at some point. Finally, that day came and I wondered how I would be able to make the money. I decided that I only needed Galleons and Sickles and not Knuts. It would be too complicated to play if there were Knuts, too.

I spray painted multiple sheets of cardboard gold and silver—gold for Galleons and silver for Sickles. Another reason not to have Knuts was that we didn't have bronze spray paint. Then I let the sheets of cardboard dry and I got a "pog" (remember those? A pog was an old, round, cardboard milk carton stopper that became a craze in the early 1990s), and I traced the circle on the cardboard. I cut the trace out and used that to make other circles. I tried to use as much of the cardboard as possible, so I drew the circles close together.

Then, for the Sickles, I used a quarter and traced it on the cardboard and cut that circle out and used it to make other circles. It took a very long time to cut the cardboard. Every night after school for about a week, I made money. I listened to Harry Potter Book One on tape as I cut the cardboard. In fact, I listened to it all the time. I listened to it so much that I had most of it memorized!

Cardboard is hard to cut because it is thick. This is what slowed me down in the process of completing my game. Finally, my family got concerned about how much time this was taking and they eventually ended up helping me. But it still took a lot of time. It was kind of strange having my mom and dad sitting around cutting out Sickles and Galleons with me. They thought I was making too many of them, but I knew that I needed to make at least 200 Galleons and 150 Sickles. I explained this to them, but they still thought it was too much. In the end, I didn't make that many. My whole entire family was glad when we were done making the money. During that week's time, I imagined that my family and I were working at Gringotts.

Now that I was done cutting it out, it was fun to have all this shiny money. After all my work, I didn't want it to just be in a cardboard box. I wanted a special container for all this money. I looked in my room for something that I could put the money in. I needed my own Gringotts. I found an old wooden box that looked a lot like a treasure chest that Harry Potter would use. I decided to use this to hold the money. I put the money in it and was ready to move on. After all, no one wants to be stuck around money too long.

11

Cloaks, Tokens, and Firebolts (Oh my!)

Money, characters, boards—my game was taking shape. But I wanted it to be more complicated. And there was more to Harry Potter than what I had already created. I got excited by all of the details in the books, such as the Invisibility Cloak, the broomsticks, the spells, and the Knight Bus. I wanted them to be a part of the game, too. But how?

In Harry Potter, the Invisibility Cloak is central to the plot. It is used in all four books. In the first Harry Potter book, Harry uses one that he got for Christmas to sneak around the school library until Argus Filch comes along and Harry runs into an empty classroom holding the mirror of Erised. Since the Invisibility Cloak is important in the books, I thought that I should have it in my game. I made four of them out of colored clay. I designed them to be able to stand up on their own. I decided that if you got an Invisibility Cloak, then you would be able to "sneak off" to the Forbidden Forest board once, whenever you chose to do so, without going to Azkaban first. In this way, the

Invisibility Cloak would work the way it does in the books—helping you avoid something you *don't* want to do or letting you do something you *do* want to do. To get an Invisibility Cloak, you would have to land on a certain space that says, "You find Invisibility Cloak."

I know there are differences between the Invisibility Cloaks in my game and in the books. For instance, in my game you can only use the Invisibility Cloak once. You can only use it for one purpose. You can also lose it by landing on a space that says, "Lose your Invisibility Cloak." And not only Harry Potter has an Invisibility Cloak in my game, but everyone can have one. I changed the nature of Invisibility Cloaks because the game would have been too easy if you got to use it as many times as you wanted. And the game wouldn't be fair if only Harry had one. The challenge in the game is to decide when the best time to use it is. That makes the game interesting.

I created Knight Bus tokens because I wanted to incorporate the Knight Bus in the game. Again, the question was how. I thought that normal buses in London had tokens, so I thought why couldn't the Knight Bus have them, too? (It turns out normal buses in London don't have tokens, but I didn't figure that out until now.) I used blue colored Sculpey clay to make the tokens and yellow clay to put the initials KB on each of the tokens. I decided that you would be able to use the tokens as a sort of "Get out of jail free" card. If you landed on a space and did not want to do what it told you, you could use your Knight Bus token to avoid doing it. Just as the tokens did with Harry, my tokens could get you out of a sticky situation. Say you landed on a square that said "Lose two Galleons." You could use the token as the Knight Bus picking you up, and so you wouldn't have to lose two Galleons. The KB token eliminated the need to follow those directions.

I decided that each player would start off with a Knight Bus token. The token could be lost, however, if the player landed on a space that said "Lose your Knight Bus token." But then it could be gotten back if you landed on a space that said, "Your owl comes back with a Knight Bus token."

Then there was the challenge of Firebolts. I thought about broomsticks and what they looked like. How was I going to make a broomstick? Well, first I decided to use toothpicks. I cut off the pointy part to make the handle and the part that you sit on. I was going to use one toothpick but that was too thin and I was worried it would break.

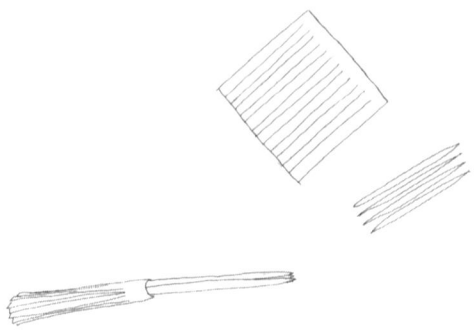

Instead, I used three toothpicks instead of one and glued them together with a glue gun. For the broom, I measured yellow paper so that it would be the right size to wrap around the "handle" of the toothpicks about three times. Then I partially cut the paper so that it was made into strands. This way it looked like the end of a broomstick. I glued the yellow part onto the toothpicks. It looked great! Everyone agreed it looked great! I made four broomsticks, because there were four players.

With the Firebolt, a person could move backwards or forward one space per turn. If they landed on the space and they didn't want to be on it or there was a space in front of them or behind them that they preferred to land on, they could use it to get away from the undesirable space or go to the more attractive space. The Firebolt could be used only five times and then the person would have to put it back in the treasure box. They could get it back by landing on a space that said "Find Firebolt." And they could lose their Firebolt by landing on a space that said "Lose Firebolt." (Of course, unless it was their fifth time using the Firebolt, they could use the Firebolt to move ahead a space and avoid landing on a square that said "Lose Firebolt"!)

In making the Cloaks, the tokens, and the Firebolts, I was discovering how to bring Harry Potter to life. By working with the things that were a part of his daily life, I made him a real part of my world.

12.
You've Got Mail

One of the main things in the Harry Potter books is the letters that are received. Letters sometimes get the characters into trouble, sometimes they help them out, and when a letter appears it is usually read immediately (except when Harry was about to turn eleven and was living on Privet Drive). In the first Harry Potter, Harry gets a letter saying he got a Nimbus 2000 and that letter was probably one of the best ones he got. But later on in that book, he gets a letter saying that his detention would happen that night at 10 o'clock. This letter got Harry into the Forbidden Forest with lots of unexpected happenings.

I loved the idea of letters and wanted my game to have letters. I thought it would make the game more interesting. So I wrote letters. Coming up with the letters was hard, but fun. It required creativity and concentration. I imagined what the different characters would say to one another.

At times, I didn't want to make the letters, but I kept on doing it. It was time consuming because I not only wrote the letters, but designed what would be on the envelopes. I thought of interesting parts of the stories and made them into stamps.

Some letters were good and gave you money or items, but some letters were bad and took away money or items. For example, I wrote a letter that I imagined Hagrid would have written to Harry inviting him to come visit him. Because Hagrid had bad handwriting, I made my letter look messy. On the back of the letter, it told you what you were to do after you read the letter. With this particular letter, it told you to go to Hagrid's shack on the Forbidden Forest Game Board. And that letter would be a good letter because it would give you a chance to get money from a quiz card.

Since Hermione is a top student, I made her writing look neat. I picked stationery that had flowers on it, and she wrote to Gilderoy Lockhart. In the letter, she hopes that he has his memory back, and I had her add a heart design at the end of the letter.

For quite a long time I tried to design a Howler. This letter would be a letter that screams out what is written. It was going to be sent to Neville by his grandmother because he had forgotten his wand, but it came with money, so it would be a good letter after opening it. I thought perhaps I could just call it a Howler and not have it scream. But I thought that I could be more creative than that and have a Howler scream. Even though I didn't have any ideas, I knew that I would get the answer in the end. I told my mom I was trying to come up with a Howler.

My mom told my dad that I was looking for a noise-maker that screams. He started looking in his desk. Let me tell you about his desk! In this desk are tons of weird, odd, strange, and fascinating items like fake dog poop, a police whistle from England, a vanishing Leprechaun, a Popeye plastic bubble blower, magnets, wood samples, buttons from the Cape Town, South Africa fire department, and pens that light up. He called me into his room and said that he had found something that might work. From his desk, he pulled out a drawer that held noisemakers. I told him I needed something that sounded like someone screaming. He pulled out an old Ghostbusters toy that sounded like a laser. I told him that that wouldn't work but that I needed something that screamed.

Then my dad pulled out another Ghostbusters toy and it had two sounds—one was a screaming sound and the other was an explosion sound. It was so small it could fit onto an envelope. This was exciting! Here was the solution! The screaming one would work in my game and my dad gave it to me.

Happy now because I had a good sound, I taped the Ghostbusters toy onto the part of the envelope that lifts up to open. I knew that when you opened the envelope it would be very hard not to press the button, so it would always go off.

When I showed my game to other kids, some got scared by it and some thought the Howler was cool. It can still be surprising when it goes off unexpectedly. Sometimes, when my mom checks on me at night, she bumps into the box that holds the Harry Potter game and the Howler goes off!

Then I made other letters, addressed the envelopes, created the stamps, and I was done. On the following pages are examples of the letters I wrote.

Since letters arrive by Owl Post, I knew that I had to incorporate owls somewhere in my game. How was I going to make owls? I didn't know. I could have made clay owls,

Dear Gildaroy Lockhart,
    I hope your memory is back.
When you feel better will you
send me a copy of <u>Mystery Me</u>
please. The money is enclosed.
        Love,
        ♡ Hermione
            Granger

Neville you forgot you wand!
There is no way I'm paying 2
Galleons to send it to you!
You buy your own!

        Your
            Grandmother

P.S. I sent 9 sickles
    for you to buy
one there!

but that seemed too hard because I didn't think I could create an owl shape. I didn't think about origami—paper folding—to make an owl, but now that seems like a good option. (I provide a pattern for an origami owl in *Journey to Gameland*. It tells you how you can create a game from *your* favorite book.) I decided to buy owls and I knew exactly where to get them. I had been to a place called The Rock Barrell many times with my father. The Rock Barrell is a store that sells a little bit of everything—rocks (of course!), minerals, fossils, thousands of beads, items made out of rocks, rock polishing supplies, and small animal figurines for necklaces. I had seen small pewter owls at The Rock Barrell and they looked exactly like the kind of owls I wanted in my game. They looked a lot better than what I felt I could make, and, because I hadn't bought anything else, I decided to buy them and use them in my game.

I added squares having to do with the letters and owls:
- Your owl gets lost.
- The Dursleys' house. Lose your owl.
- Find a letter in Moaning Myrtle's bathroom.
- Your owl comes back with a letter. Find Firebolt.

Imagining and creating the letters was even more fun than getting a letter in the mail.

13.

Are We Done Yet?

When we know how to play a game, we may take the rules for granted…until someone breaks the rules or there is a dispute over them. Then, the rules become really important. I knew I had to write rules for my game. The question was: What would they be?

As I began to think about the rules, I realized that I had made a complicated game. Compared to lots of other games, this game had a lot of components. I had to unravel what they would be and how they would work. I began by looking at the Monopoly™ rules to have an idea of organizing my rules.

The first thing rules do is they tell you the contents. So, that is what I did. I listed everything that was in the game. This turned out to be very helpful as I wrote the rules, because I could check my list to make sure that I described what each object did in the game.

Making rules involves being able to imagine people playing your game. I hadn't realized how much imagination was necessary to write the rules. But I had to anticipate all sorts of questions: How do you begin? What do you do with letters? How do you move around the board?

It took four single-spaced pages to explain how to move around the board because I had made it so complicated: Firebolts and Invisibility Cloaks and broomsticks and owls could change how someone moved.

It took a long time to write the rules. I didn't want to do it. I remember putting it off. Maybe I didn't want to do it because I didn't want to have to concentrate so hard. Like writing this book. Sometimes I don't feel like I have any ideas. I don't want to have to think. My mind feels tired. I hear it in my voice, which is impatient and a little tense. My mind wanders to happier things, like jokes my friends tell. I say, "Are we done yet?" Everything seems more attractive than focusing on the task. I pause and hope that the answer will be yes.

I guess I should say how I wrote the rules, and, for that matter, much of this book. I dictated them to my mother. At times, we would get distracted and discuss other topics. But a lot of the time we would work. This involved me, Ben, concentrating and remembering and then telling my mom what to write. When I dictated to my mom, what was fun was that I had to tell her how to spell things when usually I have to ask my mom how to spell something!

Sometimes, she would ask me questions. These would make me have to think harder or remember more. Then, I started writing. When I sat down to write I would try to concentrate and think and remember on my own.

And this is what I discovered: the rules for writing rules are a lot like the rules for writing anything—make a list of what needs to be included and stay focused. Sometimes I am surprised by how much I can remember and what I have to say. At other times, I would rather be playing the game.

Once the rules were written, I could play the game with others. And it made the frustration of writing the rules worth it. (See Appendix A for the rules I wrote for my game.)

14.
The Treasury

When I was done with all three of my boards, I began to think about what my game would come in if you bought it at a store. Even though I knew I couldn't market this game without permission from J. K. Rowling, I had to imagine how much it would cost, and even the jingle for an advertisement for it, and how it would be packaged. A box the size of a Monopoly™ box was too small to hold my game. So I thought about a box about the size of a suitcase. I started looking around the house for a box big enough for my game. I found a box that had held one of my brother's birthday gifts. It was certainly big enough to hold my game.

Because I wanted to win the Invention Convention, I wanted my box to be creative. I wanted it to leap out at people and say, "Come here and see what is here!" My dad suggested that I make my box look like a treasure chest. What a great idea! But it was complicated to do.

This was one of the few times when I needed help, and I got it. My dad and I started working on it. The challenge was to make a rounded top (like a treasure chest) that would

open from the middle. First, we attached two pieces of cardboard (B) to the top flaps of the box (A). (See drawing.) We
taped them in place so that they would form a right angle.
Now, imagine a piece of long cardboard about three times
longer than it is tall. This piece of cardboard would be the
curve of the chest. (C) With duct tape, we taped this long
piece of cardboard to the outer end of the box and to the
right angle piece of cardboard. This was hard because I had
never done something like this before, and it took a lot of
pressure to get the cardboard to curve around while also
trying to tape it into place.

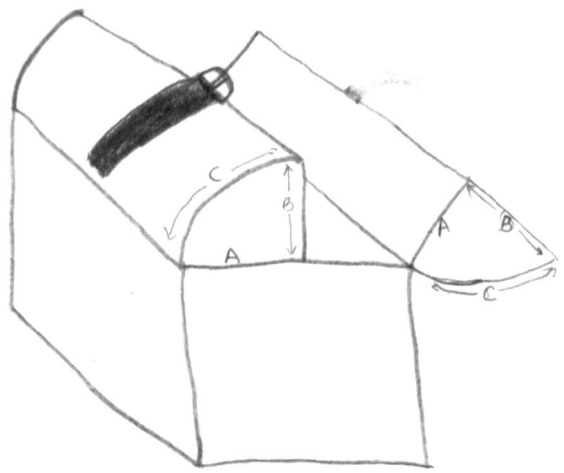

I felt excited as we worked because this was the last
thing that had to be done before the competition. I thought
about how much work I had gone through to get to this
point. When I worked by myself I listened to Harry Potter
on tape, but I couldn't do that now because I was working
with my dad. I liked working by myself, but at this point
working with someone else was easier, because I wouldn't
have been able to do it on my own. Someone had to hold

the box while someone else taped the cardboard in place. We talked about things my dad had made with cardboard when he was growing up—like a three-masted ship and a safe for his mother's Christmas present.

When we were done I spray painted the top brown, the sides, and the bottom of the box. Unfortunately, I ran out of brown spray paint so I decided to spray paint the inside silver. Next, my dad and I put duct tape on the edges so it would look more professional. Then I had the idea to cut a belt in half and glue each half onto each half of the top so the chest could be closed and locked. The treasure box was now ready to hold Harry Potter and the Search for the Lost Treasure.

Me
with the
Treasure
Chest

The Rube Goldberg Award
for Creativity

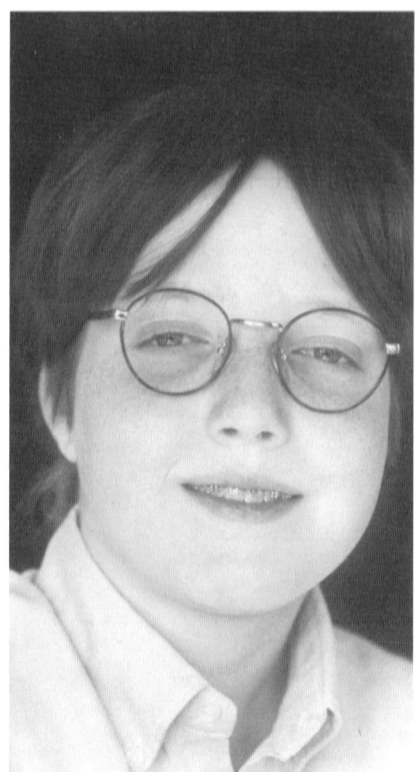

Me

Me with My Game

Me and My Game

Quidditch Dice

Quidditch Stadium

An Owl

Azkaban

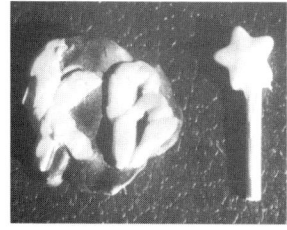

Knight Bus Token
and Wand

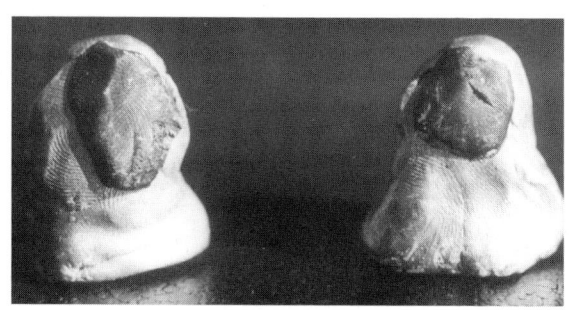

Invisibility Cloaks

Ron Weasley (left) and Harry Potter

Harry Potter

Ron Weasley and Draco Malfoy in the
Forbidden Forest and Waterfall

Draco Malfoy

Ron Weasley

Draco Malfoy on a
Quidditch Broomstick

Harry Potter
on a
Quidditch
Broomstick

The Board Game

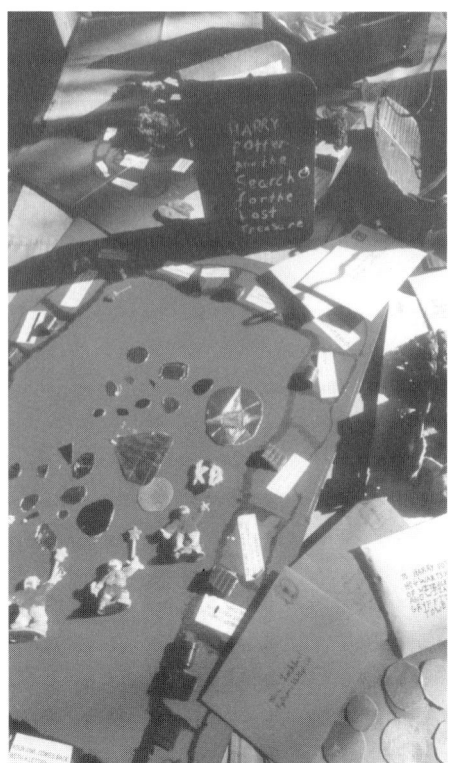

The Money Box and
Spell Scroll

The Rulebook

Photographs © Juan Garcia

15.
Mistakes: Mine and Theirs

Everyone makes ~~misteaks~~ mistakes—especially authors because they are so busy they don't have the time to check everything and when they do they are rushed, so they aren't able to catch every single thing. At least, that is what I believe by observing my mom and reading many books and now being an author myself.

In my life, I have made many mistakes, especially at school. For instance, doing homework, or quizzes, or tests. At piano, I make mistakes, but luckily there is someone there to catch them: my piano teacher. In Monopoly™—my favorite game—I make mistakes when I am trying to decide if I should buy something for a certain cost or whether or not selling something is a good trade. What I have learned from all these mistakes is that it is natural to make mistakes.

In creating the Harry Potter game, I made many mistakes. The biggest mistake I made was also the most upsetting: I had finished making the Invisibility Cloaks, the characters, and the Knight Bus tokens. I was going outside to spray them with spray enamel, which would make them stronger and keep the color, but I accidentally used the wrong spray enamel. It was the *almond* spray enamel, not the clear enamel spray. When I checked to see if they were dry, I noticed that all of the colors of the clay figurines (Ron, Harry, Malfoy, and Hermione), the Invisibility Cloaks, and the Knight Bus tokens were gone. All of their colors—red, green, brown, blue, yellow, silver, pink, black, and peach— had been destroyed! They all were *almond colored*!

I felt panicked. Now, they would all have to be painted because the colored clay that I had so carefully chosen had disappeared under the almond enamel! This might not have been a big problem, except that it was the night before the Invention Convention. I felt sad and disappointed, upset and mad. I didn't think there would be a way to fix my mistake in time and so I thought I wasn't going to be able to compete in the Invention Convention. But then my brother said that he was done with his homework, and my mom asked him if he would paint the models to restore their color. Because he was only *restoring* color that had been mistakenly covered over, it seemed okay for him to help me.

I had used so many different colors that it took even Doug a long time to paint them. This biggest mistake was probably the most painful, too, because it was so big and so dramatic and it came at the wrong time.

I made other mistakes, too. Literally, the most painful mistake that happened was that I burnt myself badly. I was gluing the gems and the jewels that I had made out of aluminum onto the Hogwarts Board. The gems conducted the heat of the glue gun and I was holding the gems! The glue gun had burned me before. The hot glue was painful. But it was not as painful as this. I had not anticipated that the aluminum jewels would magnify the heat. When I burned my fingers this way, I went into the kitchen and ran them under cold water. I put ice on them.

Probably the problem that weighed the heaviest on me was that the rocks on the Azkaban board made it too heavy! It was heavier than the other boards combined. I was worried that when I packed everything up it would break other things. My solution was that I had to take some rocks off it.

When my brother was helping me pack up the game, he folded the Forbidden Forest board too tightly so it knocked off two of the trees. I was able to glue them back on, but it didn't look as nice as before.

On the clay models that I made, I gave Malfoy brown hair when it should have been blond. I gave Harry blue eyes when they needed to be green. It's in the fourth Harry Potter that we learn that Malfoy had blond hair, and this book wasn't out yet! Also, I might have been rushing when I was making the models, so I wasn't paying full attention.

The goal I chose for the game was that the winner would have to get fifty Galleons. My mom thinks that number is too high because it would be too challenging to get that many Galleons. But I don't think it's too high.

Gilderoy Lockhart's autobiography is called *Magical Me* (Harry Potter Book Two). In the letter that I wrote from Hermione to Gilderoy, I wrote it as *Mystery Me*. It was close, but it was still wrong.

Those were some of my mistakes; now here are some of *theirs*.

The mistakes I found in Harry Potter:

I noticed that in the British edition of the first book, Professor Dumbledore asks, "Professor McGonagall would you like a sherbet lemon?" (British version, Book One, p. 6), while in the American edition, he says, "Would you like a lemon drop?" (American version, Book One, p. 8). I know that isn't a mistake. It's like saying "revising" instead of "studying." But I think the editors got confused about it. In the British edition, the password to Professor Dumbledore's office is "sherbet lemon" while in the American version it is "lemondrop." In the American version of Book Four, when Harry is trying to see Professor Dumbledore, he remembers that the password from Book Two was "sherbet lemon"(Book Four, American version, p. 557). While that was the password in Harry Potter Book Two, British version (p. 152), *it is not* the password in American version (p. 204).

Marcus Flint is a sixth year student in the first Harry Potter book (p. 185) and a seventh year student in the second book (p. 167). But he is still in the third Harry Potter book (p. 305), when he actually would have finished being a student at Hogwarts.

In the third Harry Potter book, it is said that Harry had almost been run over by the Knight Bus after he thought he saw the Grim. But it says later on that anything in the Knight Bus's way will jump out of the way. Really nobody can be run over by the Knight Bus because everything actually jumps out of its way (pages 33 and 36).

In the fourth Harry Potter on the way to the Burrow, floo powder is only used once (p. 47) even though in the second book it says that every single person has to use it (p. 48).

In Harry Potter Two, Tom Riddle says that Harry Potter is a half-blood (p. 317). But that is wrong. In all the Harry Potter books it says the father knew magic also (Three, p. 349), and we are told the mother was a witch in the first book (p. 53).

In the third Harry Potter, Mr. Weasley says to Mrs.

Weasley that Harry and Ron had ended up in the Forbidden Forest twice (p. 65), when only Harry has. Ron has only been there once.

I noticed in the Harry Potter books that even wizards make mistakes. And if wizards can make mistakes, then it seems to me that everyone can make mistakes!

16.
The Competition

The morning of the Invention Convention finally arrived. We went in early so that I could show my Harry Potter game to our librarian, Mrs. Putonti. Then we headed to the room where the inventions would be judged. It took a long time to set up the game, because it was so big, and it had so many pieces. An entire table was needed to set up my invention, and the treasure chest had to go underneath the table. It was fun to place Hermione, Harry, Ron, and Malfoy on the Board, along with all the other pieces. I arranged it so that two characters had broomsticks, and three of them had an owl. I put piles of money next to the pieces. And Knight Bus tokens went next to the piles of money.

When I finished setting up my game, I looked around to find Zein. He wasn't there. At first I was worried, but then I realized he was in the next room. We went into the other room and Zein was there setting up his invention. But a tragedy had happened! His invention had fallen on the way into the school and he was trying to glue it back together. Once again, Zein's invention had to do with storage. His invention was a pull-down attic compartment that worked so if you had a little brother or sister they couldn't get to some of your stuff. Zein had invented it because his little brother Trey always messed with his stuff. His little brother was only two, and really didn't understand the concept of respecting other people's property. Zein had created a model of what the pull-down compartment would look like. This model had rubber bands, straws, and wooden dowels inside a cardboard box that was carpeted. All these pieces made it hard to put back together.

While Zein worked to get his invention back together, I played with Trey. Now other inventions were arriving. I could see the kids setting up their inventions as Trey and I played. I was excited. I knew how hard I had worked and I felt that I had created something really great. I wondered, what had the other kids created? I would find out soon enough.

The next step was to describe your inventions to your fellow inventors and the teachers. When I began to explain my game, I picked up the pieces as I explained it. Most of the kids had been reading Harry Potter. They asked me lots of questions like "How long did it take you to make the game?" "Which is your favorite Harry Potter book?" I had listed my proposed cost for the game in both British and American money. They asked me how many pounds were in a dollar. Then it was someone else's turn to describe their invention. We went around, and there was energy everywhere as kids presented their inventions.

Later that day, our inventions were judged. We left for home but we did not know who had won. I was pretty convinced that I would win, but I wasn't 100 percent sure, so I felt eager to find out who had won. That person would go on to the next level of competition.

The Sunday after we had presented our inventions, we received a call from one of the teachers. My mom said the teacher had called to talk about a field trip. Only later did I find out that that was not the real reason why she had called. She had called to tell my parents who had won and that the winners would be announced in the morning assembly at school. This way my parents could come to the assembly, but they were asked not to tell me anything. I went to school the next morning not knowing who had won and not knowing that my mom and dad knew who had won.

At the morning assembly, all the inventors were supposed to go up to the front of our gym where our assembly was held, and the winners were going to be announced. Zein and I went up together because we were in the same class. They started with the first graders, announcing the three winners. When they finally got to the fifth graders, I was nervous. They announced the winners for third and second place. My name was not announced. I felt sad because I hadn't won third or second. At this point, I wasn't feeling so hopeful. I would rather have won second or third place than win nothing. My stomach felt like I was riding on the Hogwarts Express and it had come to a sudden stop. It felt like a Dementor had sucked out everything but nervousness from my body! Then they announced that there had been a tie for first place. I felt happy for the two people who had won, but I did not think that I was one of them. I guess I had lost my confidence in myself. Then I heard the names: Ben Buchanan and Zein Nakhoda! Now, I was as excited as Harry had felt when he won the Quidditch Cup for Gryffindor. He said he could have performed the best Patronus ever. I was glad that both Zein and I had won. I went to get my award.

Suddenly, the assembly was over and we had to go back to our classes. Seven hundred and fifty nine people left the gymnasium and headed to their homerooms. I didn't want to think about schoolwork instead of Harry Potter, but I didn't have a choice. Harry Potter would have to wait.

JUDGING FORM

Number _____   Name of Inventor _Ben Buchanan_
Name of Invention _The Harry Potter Game_

Judges will rate each category on the appropriate scale. Totals of all scores will then be added and divided by the number of judges to obtain a total score.

Already available				Re-Application			Collection of known things			Unique
0	1	2	3	4	5	6	7	8	9	10

1. Is this invention unique?   10/10/10   (0-10 pts.)

2. Is the invention useful?   10/10/10   (0-10 pts.)
     *actually operational

Unsatisfactory		Fair	Average		Good		Excellent
0	1	2	3		4		5

3. Has the inventor performed adequate research?   5/4/4   (0-5 pts.)
     *product research   [similar products]
     *market research   [reasonable price]
     *quality of research [effort exerted]
     *journal kept   [detailed]

4. Is the invention well designed/constructed?   5/5/5   (0-5 pts.)
     *by student
     *working

Unsatisfactory		Good		Excellent
0	1	2		3

5. Is their evidence of a marketing plan?   3/3/3   (0-3 pts.)
     *advertisement/jingle
     *price

6. Is the presentation exciting and effective?   2/3/3   (0-3 pts.)
     *neat & organized
     *product packaging

                                    TOTAL SCORE   _____

* Points to consider for superior or excellent ratings.

17.
The Unexpected Task

We had a month to fine-tune our inventions and make them even better before the next level of competition. But I knew that now it would be even harder to win because I would still be competing against Zein and many others inventors who had won first place or tied for first place at *their* schools.

I wanted to make the game better so that it would win at the next competition. The question was what I could do to make it better. It was hard to think of the specific things that needed improving or to be added.

As I thought about it, though, I realized I had left out some important aspects of Harry Potter's life, like spells. I wanted to include this and other stuff that I had not so far put into my game. But I never imagined making a fourth game board!

It was then that I decided that Quidditch was missing from my game. So I decided to make a Quidditch board. This was the beginning of the unexpected tasks.

I designed the Quidditch board to resemble what I thought a Quidditch stadium would look like. I cut an open-faced cylinder—like an ellipse or three-dimensional oval—out of cardboard and spray painted it gold. Another piece of cardboard I spray painted green. I glued the open-faced cylinder onto the green board so that it was standing up. This was the Quidditch stadium. I cut four pieces of cardboard into shapes that would fit into the cylinder to make seats. I colored the four pieces of cardboard for the four houses of Hogwarts: one blue, one green, one yellow, and one red. Then I drew black lines on them for seats.

I used pipe cleaners for the fifty-foot hoops. I took two green and two red pipe cleaners and made one end into a circle so that it could be the Quidditch hoops. The other end I fastened to the board.

I had some samples of plastic wood finish stains (about three inches by five inches) that were in a binder that cost a dollar at a garage sale. I glued them together to make a broom shed and placed the broom shed on the corner of the Quidditch board outside of the stadium. I made a couple more brooms to place by the broom shed.

I like solving problems. For example, I wanted to figure out how we could *play* the game of Quidditch. I was thinking that there had to be a way for the people who were playing Quidditch to know what happened on their turn. I came up with the idea of Quidditch dice. I thought of a pattern for the dice. Then I cut out six squares and I colored them in—one side was the Snitch, two sides for the Bludger, one side for the Quaffle, two sides for "nothing happens." I taped all of the pieces together. When I was testing the dice I discovered that I had accidentally weighted the dice so it almost never landed on the Snitch. This seemed appropriate, since in Quidditch matches the Seeker doesn't catch the Snitch that often.

When you go to the Quidditch board, you pick who you want to play against, then you roll the dice. If you get a Bludger you lose 10 points. If you roll "nothing happens," then nothing happens! And if you roll a Quaffle you get 10 points. If you roll the Snitch, the game would end and you would get 150 points. At the end of the Quidditch game, you get Sickles or Galleons for the points that you won. If you earned 50 points then you would receive five Sickles. If you got 100 points, you would get a Galleon.

As I worked on the Quidditch board, I thought about winning at the next competition. I wanted to win. Since I could make other changes to improve my invention at this time, I asked myself why I couldn't add spells. But how?

I made a scroll of spells. On this I put all the spells that were in the first three Harry Potter books—from *Wingardium Leviosa* to *Lumis*. To make the scroll look like a scroll Harry would use, I used some material that looked like parchment that my dad had gotten at a garage sale. I wrote the spells on this material and I glued a chopstick to each end of the scroll so it could roll up, the way scrolls do. This would make it look more realistic. (I cut off one end of each chopstick so that it wouldn't be too long.)

A wand lets you perform spells, so I made some wands. I made four wands since there are four different characters. At the church that my dad works at, nearly everyone had received a jar of candy. When this happened, I was thinking about what I could use as wands. I thought about just painting toothpicks, but I thought that wouldn't work because it probably wouldn't look like a wand. The next time I went to church, I noticed that someone had a jar of candy that had little star candies in it. I thought, "Maybe I could use the star candies as the top of the wand." The next Sunday, I asked the person who had the star candy if I could have four of the pieces. She told me I could. When I got home that Sunday, I glued them onto four toothpicks that I had cut the sharp end off of.

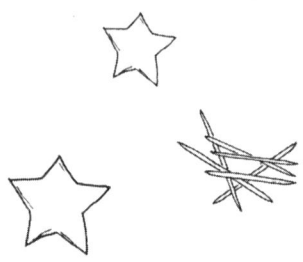

In my game, you start off with a wand but you can lose it. You need to have a wand to say a spell. You also need to know how to say the spell correctly and when to use it. For instance, if there is a spell where you said "Mumbo-Jumbo" and you thought of a house of paper clips and it let you move to any place, then you could say "Mumbo-Jumbo," and think of a house of paper clips and go to anywhere on the board. If the spell you perform is a spell that makes an object fly, then you might be able to jump ahead or back five to ten spaces. You can decide how far you want to jump. If it is a spell that lights up your wand, then nothing happens. If it is a spell that scares away a Dementor, then you may get out of Azkaban for free. You could only use a jinx spell during a Quidditch game and then your opponent would lose two turns.

In my game, when you had used all the spells once, you lost your wand. If you found a wand during the game, you could use all the spells over again.

I didn't have a rulebook like most games have, just a printed out sheet of instructions. And I had to update my

rules to include the unexpected tasks. The rules were getting long, so it seemed right to put them in a rulebook.
And it wasn't just any rulebook but a Harry Potter rulebook!

I decided that the rulebook should look like an old
book that Harry Potter himself would read or write on.
Harry Potter writes on parchment, so I glued the rules onto
the same parchment-like material that I used for the spells.
I even created an index to the rules, since they were so long!
I spray painted one side of the cardboard brown and one
side silver. The brown side became the cover, and the other
side became the inside of the book. On the cover I wrote
"Harry Potter and the Search for the Lost Treasure." On the
side, I wrote "Harry Potter." Using a special stapler with
extra big staples, I stapled the pages together. Then, using
duct tape, I put the pages into the rulebook. With my dad's
clasp-maker machine, we put a snap on a green cloth strap
and the catch for the snap on the rulebook so that it would
close and look old. Making the rulebook might sound easy,
but it wasn't.

During this time, I discovered that there are unexpected tasks everywhere. You just have to deal with them as you
go along.

18.
The Rematch

The day came for the second round of the Invention Convention. That day, around 7:30 a.m., I packed the game up and my display board that gave information on my game and left for the Invention Convention. When I got there, I went to get my Invention Convention t-shirt. We waited a long time in line because a lot of kids were there. I entered the cafeteria—I was surprised by how big it was! Everywhere I looked kids were setting up their inventions. What a noisy place it was! I saw Zein setting up his invention. Luckily, the invention was still in one piece. It turned out that the place where I was to set up my invention was right next to Zein! I felt glad about that.

All around us were other inventions: one girl had invented a certain type of thermometer. Another girl had invented a desk that could unfold out of your backpack so you could work anywhere. And one boy had invented a thing that would cover your backpack so it wouldn't get wet.

The judges were walking around the huge room and I couldn't wait to talk with them! Just when I thought they were coming to me they went to the thermometer girl, who was to my left. When Zein's turn came, I listened to how he presented his invention so I could get some ideas on how I could present my Harry Potter game. Zein talked about how his little brother Trey always got into his things and he was sure kids everywhere had the same problem as he did and that was why he had invented what he had invented.

The girl who had invented the thermometer thing had invented a cover that slipped onto the thermometer so that when the thermometer was in your mouth you would have the flavor of blueberry or cherry in your mouth, too. After she presented her invention to the judges and was packing up to leave she broke one of the thermometers and most of the mercury poured out. Little globs of mercury were every-where. I was worried that mercury would get on my game. She scooped the mercury right up in her hand and went to throw it away. She left without even washing her hands! Zein and I were concerned because mercury is dangerous. It wasn't just that it might have gotten onto our inventions, it was also that we knew you shouldn't handle mercury.

Before it was Zein's or my turn, the girls who had invented the desk backpack wanted to see the rulebook for my game. I hadn't let them because they seemed kind of wild and I was concerned they might break it. Somehow, they took it from me. They broke the clasp on the rulebook and I couldn't get it fixed. I was mad!

Now, everyone had left except for me, another inventor (who had made a volleyball velcro thing), the judges, and Zein's family. Zein's family were coming over to my house afterwards and were outside the cafeteria waiting for me.

I thought the judges were coming to me but it turned out that I was going to be last: The judges went to the volleyball velcro girl. Then she left. Now I was the only kid left in the room with the judges. The judges went to the middle of the room and talked. I could see the window and see Zein and his mom and sister waiting for me. The big room was empty now as I waited for the judges, excited and nervous.

I knew there were different prizes that were to be given. One was an environmental prize for the person who had an invention that would help the environment. One was a Container Store prize for the person who had the best storage invention. I dreamed of winning the best prize—the most patentable invention. The winner of this prize received free legal assistance from a big Dallas law firm in patenting their game. I had talked with my family about this award and I knew that I didn't own the copyright to Harry Potter and this would be a problem. Even though my game was excellent, this copyright issue might keep me from winning the award.

If I didn't win most patentable I was hoping I would at least win one of the other prizes: a critical thinking medal, the Rube Goldberg Award for Creativity, or the Best of Show Award, which is voted on by the kids. I thought about these awards as I awaited the judges.

When the judges came to me I sang my jingle ("Help Harry Potter find the lost treasure! So buy this game for your magical pleasure!") and showed them the commercial I had written for my game. It was:

Attention, Attention, Harry Potter fans!

There's a new game out for Harry Potter lovers everywhere! Now you can visit Hogwarts and the Forbidden Forest, even Azkaban!

Now you *can have broomsticks and Invisibility Cloaks, even
Howlers, just like in the Harry Potter books.*
Now you *can be Ronald Weasley, Harry Potter, Draco
Malfoy and Hermione Granger!*
Now you'll *get quizzed about how much you know about
Earth's favorite book, the Harry Potter series.*
Now you *can collect Galleons and Sickles and even take the
Knight Bus!"*

The judges asked me what problem my game addressed
and what the solution was. I taught them how to play and
I gave them my "Inventor's Folder"—where I had recorded
the steps of inventing the game. I told them that the reason
I had invented my game was because I really liked
Monopoly™ and I always wanted to play it but my friends
and family didn't like it that much. But, I said, my family
and friends *do* like Harry Potter a lot so I wondered what
would happen if I combined Harry Potter and
Monopoly™ together into one game. I explained who the
users would be and what materials I used.

I had to prove that the game was marketable. On the
display board, I had written, "I know people will like this
game because when my teacher read Harry Potter to the
class everyone loved it and everyone wanted her to read the
sequel. Everywhere, everyone is wanting to have another
Harry Potter book out, or another Harry Potter item out so
they can buy it and enjoy it. I know people will like this
game because all of the Harry Potter books have taken over
the first, second, and third places on the *New York Times* best
seller list. The first book has been on the list for 43 weeks!
The second book has been on it for 18 weeks! And the
third book has been on it for four weeks!" To prove it I had

a copy of the *New York Times* best seller list. (That was before the *New York Times* created a children's best seller list because of the Harry Potter books.)

I explained to the judges that I knew about the copyright issue with my game and Harry Potter. After I presented my game to them I went out of the room, relieved to be done. Zein's family met me. We talked about how it had gone and whether or not we thought we were going to win (I thought that I might win). We went to my house for pizza and, after we ate, Zein, my brother Doug, Zein's little sister Maria, Trey, and I all made a car out of toys called Omagles. Trey and Maria took turns riding in the car while Zein, Doug, and I took turns pushing them. We had a lot of pent-up energy!

Then my family and Zein's all went to the Invention Convention room and packed up our inventions and put them in our cars. We headed to the auditorium where the awards would be presented and right when we sat down they started to announce the awards. Now I was nervous and excited *and* hopeful. They started at the Kindergarten level and it seemed like it took a millennium for them to get to fifth grade. First, they announced the critical thinking awards and I did not win one of those, but Zein did. Then came the Rube Goldberg Awards for Creativity. They called out Zein's name. Then they called out someone else's and that name was mine! "From Hamiliton Park Pacesetter Magnet Elementary School, Ben Buchanan." I was so excited and glad that I had won. I followed Zein to the stage and we each got our awards.

Then they announced the other awards. Zein had won the Container Store award. The Best of Show Award went to two kids who had created a Pokémon™ organizer folder.

Pokémon™ had beaten Harry Potter! (But not for long!) The most patentable award was given to two girls who had invented "Math Rummy." It made me feel sad because I really liked my game and wished it could have been patented. But at least I got to keep my game!

As we were driving home, I thought, "It's over and I can't wait till next year."

19.
Searching for Treasure

When the children's librarian at my public library heard about the Harry Potter game, she asked me if I would set it up at our library in the big display window. It had now been a year since I had gotten the first Harry Potter book. Christmastime had come again. I was a year older.

We made labels for everything in my game (for instance, "the Hogwarts Board," "the Knight Bus token," "Invisibility Cloaks") so that people would know what they were looking at. After we made those labels, we went to the library to set it up. It was a windy winter day as we unloaded the treasure chest from the car.

Putting everything in the display window was time consuming. I set up my game as if it were being played. I mounted the quiz cards on the wall, and I opened some letters and mounted them. People stared at me, wondering what I was doing. When we put the letters in the window, we accidentally set the Howler off and since we were in a library everyone was supposed to be quiet. With the Howler making so much noise, it was anything but quiet!

Finally, I put the rulebook for "Harry Potter and the

Search for the Lost Treasure" in place and I was done. While my game was on display, kids would come up to the children's librarian's desk and say, "I want the new Harry Potter book."

The librarians would say, "There is no new Harry Potter book. It is coming out this summer."

"No," the kids insisted. "You have it in your window! It's *Harry Potter and the Search for the Lost Treasure.*" They thought my rulebook was the next Harry Potter! They were searching for the treasure of a new Harry Potter.

The experience of reading Harry Potter changed the way I read books. I thought reading was a little easier now because I had conquered big books. It also changed whether I thought a book was good or not. A good book needs just the right amount of detail. If the book has too much detail then it can lose the story line. If the book has too little detail, you can't get a good picture of what is going on, and you can't understand it completely. But J. K. Rowling had just the right amount of detail, like her description of Hagrid: "Arms like trash can lids and feet like baby dolphins" (Book One, p. 14). J. K. Rowling unlocked the treasure of books and taught me how to search for it in other books.

Now that I have read Book Four, if I were making another Harry Potter game, then I would create a Niffler board for little kids to search for treasure. The Niffler board would be a box with shiny stuff in it that was magnetic. You would create special Galleons with magnets attached to them. You would have a Niffler tied to some string tied to a stick and attached to the Niffler would be a magnet. You would lower the Niffler with your eyes covered by a special Niffler blindfold and you would see if you got any Galleons. The person who got the most Galleons would win.

Even without Nifflers, kids are searching for treasure.

20.
My Mystical Life

Mystical is something that touches you deeper than your senses. I pick up a Harry Potter book: that is my sense of touch. I read a Harry Potter book: that is my sense of sight. I listen to a Harry Potter book: that is my sense of hearing. When all this happens, I have a sense of enjoyment. And then because of J. K. Rowling's imagination, the Harry Potter books touched my heart.

Reading the books, I have felt scared, sad, happy, mad, sympathetic, excited, hateful, warm, puzzled, ecstatic, upset, disappointed, and tearful. When I started working on the game, I felt something even deeper. I felt a happiness almost deeper than I had ever felt before. The only other times I have felt this happiness were on my birthday and on Christmas. But this time the happiness was because I had found a book I enjoyed a lot and I was creating something from my imagination that was *greater* than my imagination. This is what was mystical about my life: I discovered that my imagination was more powerful than what I had ever imagined. My imagination and creativity grew because I was using them in a way I had never used them before. I had to transform what I knew and what I felt about Harry Potter and turn it into a board game.

Harry Potter touched my soul. I guess I knew that when I started having dreams about Harry Potter. After I finished the board game, I had a dream that all the Harry Potter characters from my game came to life. They got out two Sickles and started to play the game.

Epilogue:
Sharing the Treasure

The following June, my local library sponsored a "Make Your Own Harry Potter Game" based on my game. That morning, my friends Zein and Keaton arrived at my house and we loaded up the game. Then we went to my public library for me to share my game. We met the children's librarian, Susan Allison, who took us down to the program room using a special staff elevator. That staff elevator was something! The elevator was like the one in the movie *Men in Black*—you went in one door and out another. And it went down faster than the normal elevators at the library.

In the program room, we helped set up for all the kids who might come. We set up the chairs and tables, and we set up my game. Then Zein and Keaton were sent to sharpen about 100 pencils. And I worked on what I was going to say about how I created the game.

Earlier that month I had created a simplified version of my Harry Potter game. The idea was for it to fit onto a file folder. So, I made a board that had elements from Hogwarts on it like:

- Get caught by Filch, Lose 1 turn
- Halloween: Run from the Troll, Lose 2 turns
- Give Malfoy a black eye, lose 10 points
- Run from Snape, go ahead 5 spaces
- Fall off your broom, go to Hospital Wing
- Defeat Voldermort, gain 50 points
- Get sorted into houses, gain 2 spaces
- Christmas. Gain Invisibility Cloak.

The idea of this game was to acquire House points. I placed the Quidditch square in the middle of the file folder. Instead of dice, there was a spinner, which was also a Quidditch spinner and a trap door spinner. I divided a circle into eleven pie-like parts. Each was numbered one to eleven. Then I put an image of the Snitch on one of the spinner sections. The Quaffle, which I represented as a white circle, I put on four spinner sections, and the Bludger, which was a dark circle, was on six spinner sections. I drew trap doors on four sections, also.

When you play the game, the spinner performs different tasks depending on what is happening in the game. To move forward, you simply spin and go however many spaces that come up on the spinner. If you land on the "Trap door" squares, you spin the spinner and if the spinner lands on a number that has a trap door on it, then you go to that trap door that matches the number. If you land on a square that says "Play Quidditch" then you play a game of Quidditch by spinning the spinner and trying to get the Snitch.

This sample game was copied by the librarians and posted on the wall and at every table. There were designs for making the spinner arrow. Each kid would get a packet with

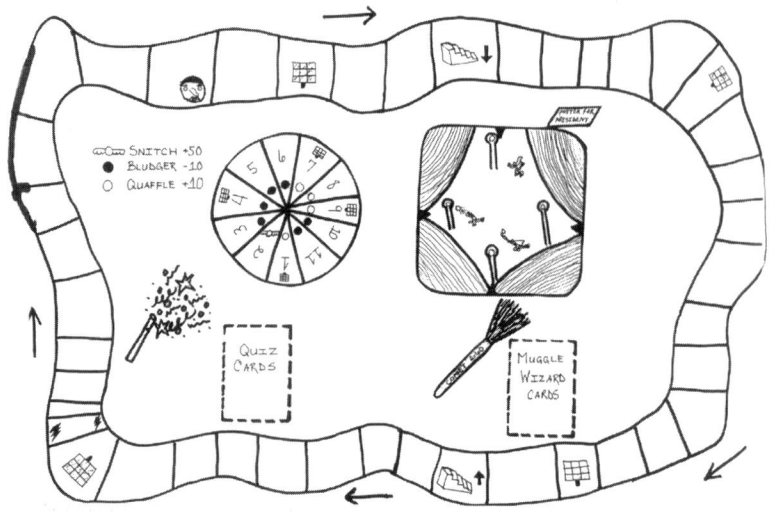

materials for making their own characters and quiz cards. There were crayons, markers, glue, scissors, and file folders at each table.

We could hear the kids gathering outside the door as we continued to get the room ready. It sounded like there were a lot of them! I started to feel nervous because I was going to have to speak about my game. Then it was time to let them in. Kids flooded in through the door. They filled up all the tables!

When all the kids settled down, Ms. Allison explained what they could do that day: they could either make their very own game or they could copy mine. She introduced me. I was excited! While I had spoken before 100 people before, it had never been about Harry Potter or me. I didn't talk long. The kids got their supplies and started to make their game.

The room was filled with a lot of excitement and talking! Many kids got right to work. The kids seemed thrilled

HARRY POTTER GAME RULES*

*Created by Ben Buchanan

The object of the game is to be the player with the most house points at the end of the game. The players (up to 4) agree to set a time limit before the game begins – the player with the most points at the end of that time wins. Everyone will start off with 5 house points. Each player will choose one of the following characters: Hermione, Ron, Harry, or Malfoy and put their character on the START space on the board. To move around the board, spin the spinner and move that number of spaces.

QUIZ CARDS. Quiz cards are cards that have a question on them about the first Harry Potter book. If you get the question correct you get the points that are on the card. You answer a quiz card each time you get to start. Note to game creator: To extend the game, try making quiz cards particular colors for each book – i.e. use blue cards to make quiz cards based on the first Harry Potter book; yellow for the 2nd book, etc. This way players can choose cards asking questions on the books they've read.

INVISIBILITY CLOAKS. If you get an invisibility cloak then you may use it once to draw a quiz card without passing start. You may sell your invisibility cloak to another player for as many points as the person you are selling it to would buy if from you or you can sell it at Broom A-Z for 5 points.

WIZARD/MUGGLE CARDS. Draw one IF YOU DARE! Card. If you land on a Wizard/Muggle space and draw a Wizard card you get 2 points; if you draw a Muggle card, you lose 1 point.

If there is a TRAP DOOR on the space that you land on, then the player who landed on that space spins the spinner and goes to a trap door if the spinner points to a trap door.

Four spaces say, "Play Quidditch." If you land on one of these spaces, pick an opponent to go to the center of the small QUIDDITCH space. The opponent has to leave their space that they are on. Once two people are in the middle of the Quidditch board, the person who was at the Quidditch board first, gets to go first. That person spins the spinner.

> *If there is a picture of the Snitch on it, then that person
>   gets 50 points and the Quidditch game ends.
> *If there is a picture of the Bludger on it, then that
>   person gets minus 10 points.
> *If there is a picture of a Quaffle on it, then that person
>   gets 10 points.

Items for the game:
- 1 Hogwarts board
- quiz cards – 10
- characters – 4
- spinner
- gold & silver "points" – 22 total, one worth 50, two worth 10, four worth 5, five worth 2, and ten worth 1.
- 2 invisibility cloaks
- Muggle/Wizard cards – 5 of each

Me posing in front of the simplified version of my Harry Potter game at the Richardson Public Library

Keaton, Zein and I working together on a Harry Potter game, the Richardson Public Library

to be making their own Harry Potter game. They were discussing and debating different aspects of Harry Potter.

Kids and their parents came to the table that had my game on it and looked at it and were amazed. One lady with really bad breath was incredibly impressed with my game. She said to me, "This is *very* interesting! My son is *very* excited by your work! You are making a *very* good example for everyone else."

One kid pointed to the Azkaban board, and asked: "Is that supposed to be Azkaban? It shouldn't be because Azkaban doesn't have walls. They're trapped in their own minds." Zein and Keaton got mad at him and Keaton said: "Do you want to try making this game?" I was pretty sure that he was wrong, but I didn't say anything just in case I was wrong. I tried to remember what I had read. Azkaban is called a fortress and Sirius Black says that he escapes from his cell doors while the Dementors were bringing food to him. (Book Three, pp. 371-2.)

I was walking from table to table looking at how people were doing and offering help. One kid said, "Did you know there are really 29 Sickles in a Galleon?" When I heard him, I was worried. I said, "Oh there are?" At first, I thought he was right; in fact I thought he was right until I wrote this chapter but when I looked it up there were 17 Sickles in a Galleon, but 29 Knuts in a Sickle (Book One, p. 72).

Most people were very respectful and thought my game was really, really awesome. They would ask questions. Like, "What is this made of?" "What are these supposed to be?" "How long did it take you to make this?"

When people were looking at the game, Zein and Keaton set off the Howler. Some people thought it was impressive, some thought it was scary. I knew that the battery was running down, so I asked them to stop.

Before I knew it, it was time to go. Two hours had gone by as if a Time-Turner had thrown us forward in time. All the kids left with their games. Zein, Keaton and I started to help clean up the room.

One last time, I packed up Harry, Hermione, Ron, and Malfoy into their wooden box. I put the Knight Bus tokens, the broomsticks, the Invisibility Cloak, and the owls in their wooden box. I folded the letters into their envelopes. I put the boards—the Quidditch, the Azkaban, the Forbidden Forest, and the Hogwarts boards—into their proper places inside the treasure chest and closed it. We went up the staff elevator and out of the library. *Harry Potter and the Search for the Lost Treasure* had ended and the treasure had been found.

Acknowledgments

I want to thank my teachers at Hamilton Park Pacesetter Magnet Elementary School for all the encouragement of my creativity. My six years at Hamilton Park have been wonderful. Thanks to Ms. Mika, Ms. Carleton, Ms. Abe, Ms. Dimijian, Ms. Barat, Ms. Hancock, and Ms. Kring for being there to teach me. My gifted teachers, Ms. Gavigan, Ms. Villanueva, Ms. Patel, Mr. Dodd, Ms. Molotsky, and Ms. Dowell stimulated my creativity. I thank my principal, Vaughn Gross, for contributing to the legacy; my school librarian, Ms. Putonti, for loaning me Harry Potter Book Three; and the Richardson Independent School District for sponsoring the Invention Convention. For help learning to read I want to thank Ms. Carol Nelson and Ms. Marcy Jones, my academic language therapists, and Ms. Nell Carvell for helping my mom find them.

I also want to thank:
- The owner of the Enchanted Forest Children's Bookstore, Jennifer Anglin, for getting my mom the

first Harry Potter—when they were so hard to get—so that she could give it to me for Christmas.

- Susan Allison and the Richardson Public Library for letting me present my game at the library.
- My friends Zein Nakhoda, Keaton Mai, Greg Holland, and Quinn Wenning for going to Hamilton Park and being my friends.
- Dr. Eisenstein for my glasses.
- Juan Garcia for taking the pictures of me and my game.
- My dad for helping me with my game and problem solving in life.
- My brother, Douglas, for helping me after a mistake and at other times.
- My mom for helping me write this book and type it.
- Aunt Nancy, Aunt Jane, Grandma and Grandpa Adams, and Grandma Buchanan—they know why.
- The RISE Foundation and Nortel Networks for sponsoring the RISD Invention Convention.
- David Dodd for letting me reprint the Invention Convention Judging Form.

Harry Potter and the Search for the Lost Treasure

Game Rules

An adventure game for four players with four different, three-dimensional, playing boards.

WARNING

If you have not read Harry Potter books one, two, and three it will be hard to play and understand this game.

CONTENTS

- *1 red Hogwarts board*
- *1 gray and green Azkaban board*
- *1 green Forbidden Forest board*
- *1 green and red Quidditch board*
- *Quidditch dice*
- *30 quiz cards*
- *4 characters*
- *20-sided and 6-sided dice*
- *140 Sickles and 179 Galleons in a treasure chest*

- *4 owls*
- *10 letters*
- *1 waterfall card holder*
- *4 Knight Bus tokens*
- *4 Firebolts*
- *4 Invisibility Cloaks*
- *Treasure chest to store owls and brooms*
- *Book of rules which you are holding in your hand*
- *1 scroll of spells*
- *4 wands*
- *copies of the Harry Potter books.*

All kept in a treasure chest box.

THE OBJECT OF THE GAME

The object of the game is to be the first player to collect 50 Galleons.

TO BEGIN THE GAME

Everyone will start off with two Galleons and one Sickle, one owl, one wand, and one Knight Bus token. Each player will choose one of the following characters: Hermione, Ron, Harry, or Malfoy and put their character on the Start space on the Red Hogwarts Board.

The quiz cards are placed behind the waterfall in the Waterfall Quiz Card holder on the Forbidden Forest Board.

Roll the 20-sided dice to see who goes first.

THE ITEMS THAT YOU CAN POSSESS

- **Letters.** To get a letter your owl either brings you one or you find one. Then you open it and read it and do what is on the back of the letter. Then the letter is closed, someone puts in the amount of money that was in there originally, if any, and it is put back.

- **A Knight Bus token.** The Knight Bus tokens let you not to have to do something that you are instructed to do. It can be used only once and then it is put back in the box, unless your owl comes and gives you one.

- **A Firebolt.** If you get a Firebolt, each turn you may move one additional space if you wish. But if you are in Azkaban, you cannot get out of Azkaban using the Firebolt.

- **Invisibility Cloaks.** If you get an Invisibility Cloak then you may use it once to go directly to the Forbidden Forest from where you are.

- **A wand.** A wand lets you perform spells, if you are saying the spell correctly and you know what it does. For instance, if there was a spell where you said "Mumbo-Jumbo" and you thought of a house of paper clips and it let you move to anyplace, then you could say "Mumbo-Jumbo," and think of a house of paper clips and go to anywhere on the board. If the spell you perform is a spell that makes an object fly, then you may jump ahead or back five to ten spaces. You can decide how far you want to jump. If it is a spell that lights up your wand, then nothing happens. If it is a spell that scares away a Dementor, then you may get out of Azkaban for free. You may only use a jinx spell during a Quidditch game and your opponent loses two turns. **You may only use each spell once.**

You may sell your Knight Bus token, your Invisibility Cloak, or your Firebolt to another player.

MOVING AROUND THE BOARDS

To move around the board the player who is controlling the character rolls a 20-sided dice and moves that amount of spaces.

- If players land on a space with a **chest**, they can choose to open it or they can choose not to open it. If they choose to open it and there are jewels in the chest then that player gains one Galleon. If Aragog the spider is in the chest they will lose one Galleon.
- If players land on a space with a **stairway** on it, they take the stair and go **directly** across the board to the other side where there is another stair.
- If there is a **trap door** on the space that they land on, then the player who lands on that space rolls a six-sided dice and goes to a trap door that matches the number on the dice they rolled. But if they roll a six, then they re-roll the dice until they get a number that is not a six.
- If they land on the **Gringotts** space they may exchange seventeen Sickles for one Galleon.
- If they go past the **"Go to Azkaban"** space they go to the Azkaban board.
- To get out of **Azkaban**, the player must pay five Sickles.
- When the player gets out of Azkaban, he or she goes to the center of the **Quidditch Board** and picks an opponent to go to the center of the Quidditch Board also. The opponent has to leave their space that they are on, even if they are in Azkaban, and go to the Quidditch Board.
- Once two people are in the middle of the **Quidditch Board**, the person who was at the Quidditch Board first, gets to go first. That person rolls the Quidditch dice to see what happens on their turn.

- If there is a picture of the **Snitch** on it, then that person gets 150 points and the Quidditch game ends.
- If there is a picture of the **Bludger** on it, then that person loses 10 points.
- If there is a picture of a **Quaffle** on it, then that person gets 10 points.
- If there is a picture of a **Question Mark in a cloud**, then nothing happens for that turn.
- When someone has rolled the **Snitch**, and the game ends, you get one Sickle for every 10 points you have, but if you have 100 points you get a Galleon. The person who rolls the Snitch and has 150 points, will get one Galleon and 5 Sickles, plus whatever else that person had in points.

- After the Quidditch game is over, the winner goes to the start of the **Forbidden Forest Board** and the loser goes to the start on the **Hogwarts Board**.
- When the player gets to the middle tree of the **Forbidden Forest Board**, another player takes a quiz card and asks the player that is in the middle of the Forbidden Forest the question that is on the quiz card. If the player gives the correct answer, he or she collects the amount of money that the card indicates. If they get the answer wrong, they have to pay 5 Sickles to each player.
- After they answer the quiz card, the player goes back to **Start** on the Hogwarts Board.
- If players land on the space that says **"find Firebolt,"** they collect a broomstick and after they roll the dice for their succeeding turns they may choose to go ahead one more space if they wish because they have the Firebolt. If they lose the Firebolt on a turn, then they cannot go ahead a space.

- If you land on a space that says **"find Invisibility Cloak"** you gain an Invisibility Cloak. An Invisibility Cloak lets you visit the Forbidden Forest **without** landing on a "go to Azkaban" space and **without** going to Azkaban once. Before they roll the dice, the player has to declare that they are going to the Forbidden Forest.
- If you land on a space that says **"Your owl gets lost"** then you lose your owl. If you still have your owl and you land on a space that says **"Your owl comes back"** you pretend that your owl was gone.
- If you land on a space that you don't want to do what the space is instructing you to do, then you may use your **Knight Bus token** once to cancel out the instructions. After you use the Knight Bus token, you must return it to the treasure chest.
- If you land on a space that says **you find a letter** or **your owl brings you a letter**, then you take a letter randomly with your eyes closed from the treasure chest. Then you can open it and read the letter and after you finish reading what is on the letter, turn it over and do what is instructed on the back.

ANSWERS TO QUIZ CARDS

1. *Bill, Charlie, Percy, Fred, George, and Ron.*
2. *935 Knuts.*
3. *Yes.*
4. *Because he put his foot through it when his TV program was canceled.*
5. *Earwax.*
6. *He works at Gringotts.*
7. *32.*

8. *713.*
9. *Platform 9 3/4.*
10. *Cursed.*
11. *Lily Potter and James Potter.*
12. *Tom Marvolo Riddle.*
13. *The Burrow.*
14. *The Polyjuice potion.*
15. *Chaser.*
16. *Nimbus 2001.*
17. *He is the Slytherin Captain.*
18. *Dobby.*
19. *Albus.*
20. *It is in Hogsmeade.*
21. *Peter Pettigrew.*
22. *It is something that spins and whistles when somebody close to you is untrustworthy.*
23. *It is a map that tells all of the secret passages in Hogwarts.*
24. *Sirius Black.*
25. *He is a Hippogriff.*
26. *Lupin, Peter Pettigrew, and Sirius Black.*
27. *You have to pet it.*
28. *Professor Lupin.*

If Your Child is Having Difficulty Reading

By Ben's Mom

Undiagnosed dyslexia is a terrible burden on a child. In fact, dyslexia is painful for the entire family. Misreading or inability to read may be interpreted as a behavioral problem instead of what it actually is: a written language disability. During first and second grade when children are learning to read, the onus on a child who can't read may feel terrible. I wish that I had understood that Ben's incapacity in first grade was because of dyslexia. I recall nights of listening to him read, as he struggled with words such as "bridge" and feeling impatient or frustrated. I could not understand why he might have been able to sound out the word on one page and then struggle all over again with the word on the next page.

Dyslexia is called a hidden disability—there is no way to see it if you look at the child. The problem becomes even more complicated if your child is gifted. They will be acutely aware that they are not performing at the level they expect themselves to. And because of their intellectual skills, they may actually be functioning at the grade level, even though for them they are performing below their skill level. You cannot expect that your school will necessarily identify your child's dyslexia.

Because children in third grade are now reading to learn, rather than learning to read, the importance of reading to the third grade curriculum can be even more overwhelming to a child. It is presumed that basic reading skills have been achieved; for the dyslexic, this is not true.

I knew nothing about dyslexia. I also knew very little about the process of learning to read. My basic philosophy was that the alphabet was a symbol system that schools were equipped to teach. Why rush into reading when the preschool and kindergarten child had so many other rich experiences available to them? I read to my children every night, and found that to be an incredibly wonderful experience. I was in no hurry to be displaced from that role and left it to the elementary school to teach each of my children how to read. For our first child, there was no problem and by the middle of first grade he was reading. But Ben clearly was having difficulties. I assumed it was simply because he needed more time to learn how to read, and any intuitions that there was something else wrong were silenced in the face of slow, frustrating, but slightly visible progress. Now I understand that dyslexia can be identified in kindergarten, and I wish that we had been able to offer that to Ben. Only when Ben's gifted teacher reported that his reading and writing skills were clearly lagging behind his peers in May of his first grade year, did that galvanize me into action. I had needed confirmation for my feelings of concern.

I was fortunate in having a friend, Nell Carvell, whose expertise is dyslexia and the public school system. Without her, both the identification and the remedy would have been much longer to achieve, and anything that would have postponed intervention, I believe, would have harmed Ben's self-esteem considerably.

The first step is to have an assessment. Depending on your state law, your schools may be required to provide assessment of your child. Because it was near the end of school, the school system deferred doing the needed testing until the beginning of second grade. I could have insisted on the testing happening in May, but I had already decided to follow Nell's second advice, to have Ben begin the alphabetic-phonics tutoring program in which an academic language therapist would work one-on-one with Ben for one hour each weekday. After the six weeks of work with Carol Nelson—an academic language therapist Nell referred us to—Ben's reading had advanced so rapidly I was an immediate and heartfelt convert to that program.

When second grade began, the assessment occurred. It is important that you know how to interpret the tests that are used in an assessment. Don't let others simply tell you what they mean. The most helpful book on this subject for me was Priscilla Vail's *Smart Kids with School Problems*. (Read everything by this woman you can get your hand on, especially *About Dyslexia: Unraveling the Myth!*) You must be alert to the fact that an achievement test may show that your child is functioning at his grade level, and so the school will decide there is nothing they can do. But your child may be performing at grade level and yet you sense there is a problem: Are you surprised that your child is working so hard to get the grades she is getting? Is he having to exert much more effort than his peers just to keep up at school?

Testing for dyslexia can also be provided by a licensed

diagnostician or an educational psychologist. They will administer a full battery of tests—looking at the whole child. When this testing confirmed that Ben was dyslexic, we worked with the school to pull Ben out of his classes for one hour each day to continue with the alphabetic phonics program. From the middle of second grade until the end of third grade, Ben followed this routine, and an academic language therapist came to the school to provide the instruction.

Ben continued to thrive in his acquisition of skills that seem to come naturally to us nondyslexic individuals. This is because the alphabetic-phonics program slowly teaches the structure of the English language and is multi-sensory, structured, and sequential—so the child succeeds every day.

When Ben identified his highlights of 1996, one of them was "going to Ms. Nelson."

Alphabetics phonics is not an inexpensive program. Tutoring fees can be onerous. If you have relatives who can help you cover these fees if your income cannot cover them, allow them to help. Helping a child achieve his or her reading potential is not only a parent's concern. It is a concern of everyone who loves and cherishes that child or any child. And there are places that provide scholarships or free remedial written language therapy. You can get more information on this program from the Academic Language Therapy Association (ALTA). They have a Helpline (972-907-3924). At this number you will speak with a member of ALTA and get information or referrals. You can also check their website: www.ALTAread.org.

Within the school system, your child needs an advocate and that advocate must be you. Create a binder. Keep all relevant material in it. Insist on your rights under state and federal law. Each state may vary in terms of what it sees as rights and responsibilities of the child and the school. You need to find out what your state establishes as those rights and responsibilities.

Dyslexic children often think three-dimensionally. They often become engineers, architects, car mechanics, and surgeons. The way that Ben engaged Harry Potter is in a sense also an aspect of his dyslexia—he made it three-dimensional.

If you have any inkling of a reading difficulty—don't delay!

To learn more about dyslexia call the International Dyslexia Association 410-296-0232, write them at 8600 LaSalle Road, Chester Building/Suite 382, Baltimore, MD 21286-2044, or check out their website at www.interdys.org. The Learning Disabilities Association is an advocacy association. You can contact them at 412-341-1515.

Extending the Magic of Harry Potter

My librarian gave me a list of good books similar to the Harry Potter series, that I could read as I waited for the next book from J. K. Rowling. Here it is:

Alexander, Lloyd. *The Book of Three.* New York: Holt, 1999.

——.*The Remarkable Journey of Prince Jen.* New York: Dutton, 1991.

Baker, Betty. *Seven Spells to Farewell.* New York: Macmillan, 1982.

Belden, Wilanne. *Frankie!* San Diego: Harcourt Brace Jovanovich, 1987.

Bradshaw, Gillian. *Beyond the North Wind.* New York: Greenwillow, 1993.

Brittain, Bill. *The Mystery of the Several Sevens.* New York: HarperCollins, 1994

Buchwald, Emilie. *Gildaen.* New York: Harcourt Brace Jovanovich, 1973.

Charnas, Susan McKee. *The Bronze King.* Boston: Houghton Mifflin, 1985.

Chetwin, Grace. *Gom on Windy Mountain*. New York: Lothorp, Lee & Shepard, 1986.

Chew, Ruth. *Do-It-Yourself Magic*. New York: Scholastic, 1987.

Cooper, Susan. *The Dark is Rising*. New York: Atheneum, 1974.

Corbett, Scott. *Dr. Merlin's Magic Shop*. Boston: Little, Brown, 1973.

Coville, Bruce. *Jeremy Thatcher, Dragon Hatcher*. San Diego: Harcourt Brace & Co., 1991.

Cunningham, Julia. *Oaf*. New York: Knopf, 1986.

Duane, Diane. *Deep Wizardry*. San Diego: Harcourt Brace & Co., 1996.

——. *High Wizardry*. San Diego: Harcourt Brace & Co., 1997.

——. *So You Want to be a Wizard*. San Diego: Harcourt Brace & Co., 1996.

——. *A Wizard Abroad*. San Diego: Harcourt Brace & Co., 1997.

Eager, Edward. *Seven Day Magic*. New York: Harcourt Brace, 1990.

Fisher, Paul. *The Ash Staff*. New York: Atheneum, 1979.

Halam, Ann. *The Daymaker*. New York: Orchard, 1987.

Henry, Maeve. *The Witch King*. New York: Orchard, 1988.

Jones, Diana Wynne. *Archer's Goon*. New York: Greenwillow, 1984.

——. *The Lives of Christoper Chant*. New York: Greenwillow, 1988.

——. *The Magicians of Caprona*. New York: Greenwillow, 1980.

Keller, Beverly. *A Small Elderly Dragon*. New York: Lothorp, Lee, & Shepard, 1984.

LeGuin, Ursula. *A Wizard of Earthsea*. New York: Atheneum, 1991.

Lewis, C. S. *The Lion, The Witch, and The Wardrobe*. New York: HarperCollins, 1997.

Lovett, Margaret. *The Great and Terrible Quest*. New York: Holt, Rinehart, and Winston, 1967.

MacLachlan, Patricia. *Tomorrow's Wizard*. New York: Harper & Row, 1982.

Mazer, Anne. *The Accidental Witch*. New York: Hyperion, 1995.

McGowen, Tom. *The Magician's Apprentice*. New York: Dutton, 1987.

McKillip, Patricia. *The Riddlemaster of Hed*. New York: Atheneum, 1987.

Nichols, Ruth. *A Walk Out of the World*. New York: Harcourt, Brace & World, 1969.

Parker, Richard. *Spell Seven*. New York: T. Nelson, 1971.

Pierce, Tamora. *Alanna: The First Adventure*. New York: Atheneum, 1997.

——. *Briar's Book*. New York: Scholastic, 1999.

——. *Daja's Book*. New York: Scholastic, 1998.

——. *Sandry's Book*. New York: Scholastic, 1997.

——. *Tris's Book*. New York: Scholastic, 1998

Price, Susan. *Ghost Dance: The Czar's Black Angel*. New York:

Farrar, Straus, & Giroux, 1994.

Rowling, J.K. *Harry Potter and the Chamber of Secrets*. New York: Arthur A. Levine 1999.

——. *Harry Potter and the Goblet of Fire*. New York: Arthur Levine, 2000

——. *Harry Potter and the Prisoner of Azkaban*. New York: Arthur Levine, 1999

——. *Harry Potter and the Sorcerer's Stone*. New York: Arthur Levine, 1999

Service, Pamela. *Storm at the Edge of Time*. New York: Walker, 1994.

Smith, Sherwood. *Wren to the Rescue*. San Diego: Harcourt Brace Jovanovich, 1990.

Willard, Barbara. *Spell Me a Witch*. New York: Harcourt Brace Jovanovich, 1979.

Willard, Nancy. *The Sorcerer's Apprentice*. New York: Scholastic, 1993.

Yolen, Jane. *Hobby*. San Diego: Harcourt Brace, 1996

——. *Merlin*. San Diego: Harcourt Brace, 1997.

——. *Passager*. San Diego: Harcourt Brace, 1996.

——. *Wizard's Hall*. San Diego: Harcourt Brace Jovanovich, 1991.

——. *The Wizard's Map*. San Diego: Harcourt & Co., 1999.